JOHN, PAUL, GEORGE, & RINGO

Superfans

1D

Katy Perry FAN CLUB

KISS ARMY

Superfans

MUSIC'S MOST DEDICATED

FROM BEATLEMANIA TO THE BEYHIVE

1D

BY TOBIAS ANTHONY

Smith Street Books

Contents

What is a superfan?	6
AC/DC fans (AC/DC)	8
Barbz (Nicki Minaj)	12
Beatlemania (The Beatles)	16
Beliebers (Justin Bieber)	20
The BeyHive (Beyoncé)	24
Britney Army (Britney Spears)	28
Bruce Tramps (Bruce Springsteen)	32
Deadheads (Grateful Dead)	36
Directioners (One Direction)	40
Elvis Nuts (Elvis)	44
Fanilows (Barry Manilow)	48
The Juggalos (Insane Clown Posse)	52
KatyCats (Katy Perry)	56
KISS Army (KISS)	60
Lisztomania (Franz Liszt)	64
Little Monsters (Lady Gaga)	68
Maggots (Slipknot)	72
Parrotheads (Jimmy Buffett)	76
Phishheads (Phish)	80
Punkers? Robots? Dafties? (Daft Punk)	84
Rihanna Navy (Rihanna)	86
Smilers (Miley Cyrus)	90
Stans (Eminem)	94
Swifties (Taylor Swift)	98
The Victims (The Killers)	104
About the author	110

Introduction

What is a superfan?

Music touches the world and those who inhabit it in profound ways ...

Shaping culture, memories and even how we come to understand our identities. For some, though, the latter has been taken ... um ... too far?

In *Superfans*, we've gone deep into some of the music world's most obsessive fan bases in an effort to reveal just how they think, feel and behave, and why. Fair warning: There isn't always an answer ...

So, exactly what *is* a 'superfan' and how does one qualify?

Typically, we think of Elvis nuts: groups of middle-aged men in flared sequined jumpsuits who sport mutton-chop sideburns and quiffs. Or we think of the screaming Beatles fans who swarmed JFK Airport in 1964 when the most famous band of all time made their debut arrival in the United States.

But the world of modern music is now populated by a host of varied subcultural groups, all dedicated to contemporary extremes. There's pop, of course, and with it armies of devotees to the likes of Lady Gaga (Little Monsters), Justin Bieber (Beliebers) and Beyonce (the Beyhive). But, if you're not into pop, we've got you covered. We've been comprehensive in our selection, and we haven't discounted the worlds of heavy metal (Maggots) or rap (the Barbz) either. Nor have we forgotten that some people like listening to long sessions of improvisational noodling (Phishheads), while others just can't get enough of that mainstream genre known as 'horror-core' hip-hop (the Juggalos).

Regardless of your personal musical preferences, though, it's simply interesting to discover the long and storied history of music superfandom.

One wonders what the future wave of obsessives might look like ...

AC/DC fans

ACIDC

Demo

Those about to rock.

Price of admission

A highway to hell.

Signatures

Dirty deeds done dirt cheap.

Who are the AC/DC fans?

After being founded in 1973 by Scottish-born brothers Malcom and Angus Young, the Australian rock quartet AC/DC quickly became a hit in the rock scene of the era. With hectic guitar playing, most notably from Angus (always attired in his customary school-boy uniform) the band were set to take the world by storm. But, after losing their lead singer Bon Scott in 1980 – Scott died after a night of heavy alcohol consumption – it seemed like it might be over for the Aussie rockers.

And then they released *Back in Black* ...

Their 1980 album might never have been; there was a period after Scott's death when AC/DC initially considered disbanding. But this would not have been Scott's rock wish, they thought. Instead, they forged ahead with new lead vocalist Brian Johnson, and made their seminal album a tribute to their fallen soldier.

It was the right idea. With an estimated 50 million copies of the record sold worldwide since its release, *Back in Black* is the second-highest-selling album by any artist, and its release cemented the band's legacy of rock holiness, pulling in a staggering number of fans along the way.

Unlike other superfan groups in this book, AC/DC obsessives don't have a collective name. They simply call themselves AC/DC fans and let the music and the legacy of the band speak for themselves. Besides, no fan group nickname could ever top the band's actual name and its origin story. According to legend, when pint-sized guitarist Angus Young first formed the band, his sister used to make his school uniforms. On her sewing machine was a label that read AC/DC, the shorthand for alternating and direct electrical current. Young considered this the perfect name for a macho band. He still wears the schoolboy uniform on stage to this day.

While AC/DC fans don't care about having a collective name, their passion remains firmly connected to the music. The frenzied fandom was documented in the band's concert movie, *AC/DC: Live at the River Plate*, which captures their epic 2009 shows at the Buenos Aires soccer stadium, where they played to up to 200,000 rabid fans. One superfan of note is Richard Richards, whose fanaticism was ignited by an 8-track of the song 'High Voltage' and who, appropriately, works as an electrician. Since being exposed to AC/DC's music, Richards has dedicated himself to amassing a collection of band memorabilia. Most prized in his collection are his numerous tattoos that range from the fly from *Fly on the Wall*, to the words 'Hells Bells' on one elbow and 'Flick of the Switch' on his forearm as well as a silhouette of Angus Young.

Of the band, Richards says, 'I love their music. I can't explain it. Their music just clicks with me.'

Why you should become an AC/DC fan …

Because they're a bloody decent lot, that's why. And because the band appreciates just how great their fans are.

When Malcolm Young left the band in 2014 after receiving a diagnosis of dementia, the Swedish faction of AC/DC obsessives set out to raise funds for Alzheimer's research. So moved by this show of support, Brian Johnson posted a special message to the fans thanking them for their efforts: 'I just want to say, I'm so proud of what you're doing for the Alzheimer dementia research … I think what you're doing to raise awareness of everyone about this dreadful disease is just absolutely fabulous.'

But the respect doesn't end there. With more than 200 million records sold worldwide, AC/DC and their fans have the respect of the entire music business. When Johnson was ordered by a doctor not to take to the stage again during the band's 'Rock or Bust' tour, Guns N' Roses frontman Axl Rose stepped in to fill his shoes, ensuring fans wouldn't miss a chance to see the band live.

You're a top bloke, Axl!

Barbz

Nicki Minaj

Vibe

Japanese-infused girly kitsch meets gun tattoos and aggressive NY hip-hop.

Classic throwdown

@IamRossMathieu: @MariahCarey YOU ONLY DO MUSIC FOR MONEY AND FAME SO F**K YOU.

Signatures

Spending rent money on multicoloured wigs.

Famous feuds

During Nicki's time as a judge on *American Idol*, tensions with her fellow judge Mariah Carey reached boiling point. The two divas do not get along, not for a second. And Barbz everywhere were there to fan the flames.

Who are the Barbz?

After garnering early attention with three mixtapes released between 2007 and 2009, Trinidad-born New York rapper Nicki Minaj was picked up by Young Money Entertainment. Since then, Minaj's first two solo albums have peaked at number one on the U.S. Billboard 200 chart and she has produced a series of hit singles. But we're not here just to talk about one of the biggest sensations in female rap and hip-hop since the likes of Lauryn Hill (a big influence on the young Queens-raised rapper, by the way); we're here to talk about her fans: the Barbz.

However, in order to do that, we must first shed some light on the Harajuku Barbie.

'The what?' you ask. It's a fair question. Get ready...

Minaj's trademark look, which includes bubblegum-pink hair and hyper-feminine, stylised clothing such as ball gowns and tutus, is something she calls her 'Harajuku Barbie' look. A perfect example of this aesthetic can be found on the cover of her debut studio album from 2010, *Pink Friday*.

To understand the Harajuku Barbie isn't just to understand Minaj herself, but to understand her fan base, who she refers to as 'Barbz', an abbreviation and plural form of Barbie. (Nicki's male fans are called either 'Boyz' or 'Ken Barbz'.)

The Harajuku Barbie combines the Harajuku aesthetic – a youthful, colourful and playful look that has its origins in the Harajuku neighbourhood of Tokyo – with that of a Barbie doll. For Minaj, this aesthetic matches her personality, which she describes as being 'free-spirited, girls-just-wanna-have-fun, kick ass', and because, according to Minaj, 'all girls are Barbies; we all wanna play dress-up, all wanna put on lipstick and be cute and sexy', the Harajuku Barbie persona doesn't just fit her own personality but 'it happens to fit a lot of other girls' personalities' as well. For this reason, the aesthetic has taken off among her superfans. Heck, even toy company Mattel have gotten in on the act, manufacturing a custom-made Barbie modelled after Minaj, which was valued at US$15,000 at a recent auction.

By nicknaming her followers, Minaj says that it has helped strengthen their relationship: 'They feel like they're a part of a certain club, it boosts their self-esteem because they're no longer a fan, they become a friend.'

Additionally, the term 'Barbz' seems a fitting one, as it also conjures up an image of barbed wire. This mix of sweet and sour is something with which Nicki has become synonymous.

Why you should become one of the Barbz...

If Barbies aren't your thing, then how about we focus on the music? Oh, and Nicki's many adorable, adorable, adorable – *did we say adorable?* – little fans.

It's pretty much a guarantee that hits like 'Moment 4 Life', 'Starships' and 'Anaconda' will move you to dance. Truly, you'll end up thrusting and twerking like the rest of us, and might even join the ranks of Nicki's most ardent supporters, who, strangely enough, happen to be children.

Take 12-year-old Belfast wunderkind Danny McGahey. for instance. When, on her Pinkprint Tour, Minaj called several fans up from the crowd to meet her, Danny stole the show by joining in to dance and perform right alongside the other back-up dancers, twerking his booty to the packed-out arena, all before declaring Minaj the 'Queen of rap'. Afterwards, through a torrent of tears, Danny gushed, 'I've been dreaming of this moment for so long.' Fortunately, someone in the crowd captured the performance, which can be viewed online. It's well worth a watch, so check it out!

But, if that doesn't win you over – *and how could it not?* – then it's time for you to head to YouTube to join the 52 million others who have watched Sofia Grace Brownlee from Essex flawlessly perform 'Super Boss'. The viral video made her such a sensation that she wound up as a guest on *The Ellen DeGeneres Show*. See where being one of the Barbz can get you?

And hey, you might even embrace that whole Harajuku thing after all …

Beatlemania

The Beatles

Vibe

Suits, shades and bowl cuts.

Demo

All planetary lifeforms.

WE ♥ THE BEATLES

I WANT TO HOLD YOUR HAND JOHN!

BEATLE MANIAC

I LOVE RINGO

POLICE LINE — DO NOT CROSS

Willing to forgive

Everything about the writing and recording of 'Yellow Submarine', the most irritating song ever produced by a mainstream band.

What was Beatlemania?

It says a lot that a band that hasn't been together, played a show, or recorded a single piece of music in over 40 years (almost *50!*) finds itself with verified accounts on Twitter and Instagram. It says quite a lot, too, that spellcheck doesn't pick up 'Beatlemania' as a made-up or incorrect word. And the reason for all of this is simple: The Beatles are a part of history. A part of history as unlikely to be forgotten as the fall of the Berlin Wall, the bombing of Hiroshima and Nagasaki or, uh, Donald Trump's ascendency to the office of President of the United States of America.

Like Lisztomania (pages 64–67), Beatlemania is more a diagnosis than a moniker for the fans. It was a word coined to describe the frenzy of enraptured Beatles fans, such as the one that ensued, famously, when they first arrived in America. On February 7, 1964, after flying into New York, Paul McCartney, John Lennon, George Harrison and Ringo Starr, all then in their twenties, were greeted by a crowd of 3000 ecstatic, screaming fans.

(Two days later, their performance on *The Ed Sullivan Show* would smash television rating records.)

Today, much of what Beatlemania was in the 1960s has been distilled into black-and-white photos – many of them taken the day the band arrived in New York – depicting teenage girls losing their minds, crying and near passing out as they push themselves against some form of blockade designed to prevent them from tearing John, Paul, George and Ringo (well, maybe not Ringo) limb from limb.

With so much literature written about The Beatles and with so many documentaries utilising the band as subject material, Beatles lore continues to expand. And as this lore expands, Beatlemania too continues to be cultivated. For instance, there isn't a person living today who can escape picking up, subconsciously or otherwise, phrases like 'Let It Be' or 'Strawberry Fields' or … 'Yoko Ono'.

Today, Beatlemania is no longer the frenzy of an individual losing their mind over the sight of a band. It's our culture's fanatic devotion to the Beatles' legacy.

Why you should become a Beatlemaniac ...

Given that you're reading this book, we're going to take a guess that you're probably a citizen of planet Earth who was born some time within the last 100 years. If so, then chances are you've experienced some form of Beatlemania already. You don't actually need a reason. So, instead, here's a list of some people still suffering from Beatlemania today:

1) Paul Minett: In 1967, Minett stood outside Abbey Road Studios, clutching his *Sgt Pepper* LP and waiting desperately for autographs. Well, he got *some*, but only three – from Paul, George and John. For some reason, Ringo wasn't there that day and so Minett spent *30 years* waiting to complete a lifetime obsession; getting that final signature on his album. When he finally got Starr's autograph in 1997, it took the estimated value of the LP from £15,000 up to a staggering £40,000.

2) Jackie Holmes: The aptly named Holmes has made it her lifelong obsession to own the childhood homes of the Fab Four. Currently, she only owns three: Ringo and George's family homes and John's mum's house. You might be wondering what she plans to do with them, but the answer is fairly mundane: she's leasing them out.

3) Dean Johnson: Johnson spent six months recording ordinary peoples' chance meetings with The Beatles. The result was a book entitled *The Beatles and Me*, collecting 700 contributions from people across the globe on their experiences with John, Paul, George and Ringo and covering five decades of Beatlemania.

With so many people still influenced by the band that helped define not only rock 'n' roll, but the 1960s, Beatlemania is not going away anytime soon.

Beliebers

Justin Bieber

Demo

Swooning tweens and teens discovering their sexual identities.

Signature

Throwing shade at whichever celebrity's offspring Biebs is seen with, whether it be Lionel Richie's daughter or Alec Baldwin's niece.

NEVER SAY NEVER

BELIEBER

Notable dust-ups

Beliebers everywhere rushed to Justin's aid after a nasty tweet from a 15-year-old girl was retweeted by Justin himself. The tweet said: 'Not really a fan of Justin Bieber but his acoustic album is actually good!' Thankfully, the Beliebers were able to stem such savagery by bombarding the young Twitter user with death threats.

Moment of madness

A bottle of sparkling water, from which Justin took a single sip before deciding he didn't like it, was sold online for $624 to the parents of a Bieber uber-fan.

Who are the Beliebers?

In 2008 the world was treated to a series of YouTube videos showing a child performing covers on his guitar.

'What a voice!' the world cried. 'What an angel! What talent!'

'Who was this boy?' you ask. Well, none other than Justin Drew Bieber, who, since signing with RBMG Records in 2008 after his videos were discovered by a talent manager, boasts the most loyal army of adoring fans. His followers, naturally, call themselves Beliebers.

And all of this despite the fact that young Justin, who was born in 1994 (*sigh*), is Canadian. Not bad, eh?

The moniker 'Belieber', of course, is a simple portmanteau combining 'Bieber' and the word 'believe'. The word is commonly associated with the line uttered by many Beliebers, 'Once I saw his face, I was a Belieber', which is an update of the hit song 'I'm a Believer' by The Monkees. There's no great origin story here – it's a simple word and the line is catchy, but the simplicity of 'Belieber' captures the essence of what it is to be a Justin fanatic.

Since Bieber was a mere 16 years of age, his fans have been there to support him through a career that has seen him evolve from teeny-bopper/ pop icon into a serious hit-making, chart-topping machine (and master of the body roll). This musical evolution has been accompanied by the evolution of Beliebers, too, from predominantly female teeny-boppers to a more diverse audience, which is only natural seeing as his most recent collaborations have involved the likes of club powerhouses Skrillex, Diplo and DJ Snake.

Despite Bieber's troubles off the stage, the future seems bright for Beliebers, who Justin credits with recent turnarounds in attitude and career. Things should only continue to look up, so long as they continue to believe.

Why you should become a Belieber ...

Have you seen his face? Do you believe? No?

Well, if you're not a fan already, then the many online guides entitled 'How to be a Justin Bieber fan' might help. According to such Belieber-made propaganda, it's simple:

1) Don't just call yourself a 'fan', real fans are called 'Beliebers'.

2) Memorise his song lyrics.

3) Being a Belieber isn't about the merchandise, because not everyone can afford it. Many Beliebers will wear home-made T-shirts to his concerts

4) Learn the basic facts: Justin's DOB, his favourite colour (purple, FYI) and family members.

5) Show it off. Make sure everyone knows you're a Belieber. You will be teased by haters, but every true Belieber is willing to put up with this.

6) Make a Twitter fan account.

7) Respect Justin's crew. Never make fun of his bodyguard, Kenny, or his swag coach, Ryan Good, or his manager, Scooter. They're all part of your family now.

8) Try to put lots of posters of him on your bedroom wall.

And always remember, as one online Belieber reminds us: 'Just because you didn't like him from the start doesn't mean that you're not a Belieber. That's a fantasy spread by people who are way too competitive and not family oriented. The Belieber family is an open one and will accept anyone into the family. As long as you don't just like him because of the way he looks and you honestly and truly love him as a person and his music, then you're fine, welcome to the Belieber family!'

Welcome all, indeed.

The BeyHive

Beyoncé

Demo

All the
single ladies.

QUEEN BEY

Known for

Being the gatekeepers
for divas everywhere.
the BeyHive have zero
tolerance for anyone
who thinks they might
out-sass or out-glam
their Queen Bey.

Famous spats

The BeyHive are known for ravaging
other pop stars, especially those who
consider throwing shade in the direction
of their beloved Beyoncé. When singer
Chaka Khan rolled her eyes after being
compared to Beyoncé by a reporter,
the BeyHive launched an attack of
epic proportions on social media. The
slightest of slights are not tolerated by
the Hive.

What is the BeyHive?

Arguably the most creative fan group name on this list, the BeyHive serves both as a catchy *buzz* word and as a warning.

Penned by the fans themselves after shaking their heads in a unified 'no' on Twitter when 'Beyontourage' was proposed, BeyHive combines the 'Bey' from Beyoncé with the notion that her loyal fans are one collective hive-like community. And the bond in solidarity is no stronger than amongst Bey-Bey's ardent superfans. Nor are any fans out there seemingly more fierce, ferocious and passionate when it comes to looking out for their Queen.

The Hive are more than just fans, though, they're cultural assassins, waging a war in honour of the One True Diva. And the celebrity hit list of those stung by the Hive is pretty darn impressive:

Rachel Roy: When Roy alluded to a possible affair she'd had with Jay-Z on Instagram, the BeyHive littered her account with bumblebee emojis for weeks.

Rachel Ray: Mistakenly, some Killer Beys embroiled the unwitting celebrity chef in the Roy controversy – but, hey, there were always going to be casualties ...

Piers Morgan: Some Hiveminds didn't take too kindly to Mr Morgan weighing in on which era Beyoncé he preferred and dragged him through the mud on social media for deigning to so much as comment on their Queen.

Azealia Banks: When Banks described Beyoncé's *Lemonade* narrative as the antithesis of feminism, well you just know the Hive were there to deal ...

Kid Rock: When Rock suggested he didn't understand Bey-Bey's success, his social media accounts were flooded with the symbol of the Beys – that same bumblebee emoji they love so much. So bombarded was Rock by these angry Beys, that he posted a picture of a can of bug spray to his Instagram account.

Betsy McCaughey: When this former Lieutenant Governor of New York attempted to defend Donald Trump's attitudes about women, she discredited Hillary Clinton by arguing that Clinton was a hypocrite for condemning Trump given that she is a fan of Beyoncé. Naturally, the BeyHive responded and let's just say old Betsy didn't like the sting too much – her Facebook account has been private ever since …

All in all, this is one insanely loyal mob. So, you know, be wary of what you say …

Why you should become a member of the BeyHive …

If the fear of getting on the wrong side of the Hive isn't enough motivation for you, then how does 24 MTV Music Video Awards, 22 Grammys and 100 million records sold worldwide sound?

It sounds pretty damn good, let us tell you. It's the sound of 'Crazy in Love', 'Check on It', 'Irreplaceable', 'Single Ladies (Put a Ring on It)' and 'Drunk in Love'.

There's a reason the BeyHive are so passionate, you know …

Britney Army

Britney Spears

Signature

Forgiveness. Especially forgiving of their idol's diminishing talent.

Demo

Pop fans still living in the late 1990s.

The price of admission

Coming to terms with the realisation that the past is the past and that Britney's Vegas days are, well, kind of lacklustre.

▶ ▶| 🔊 1:53 / 4:17 ⚙ ▢ ⛶

Leave Britney Alone

VIP fans

Britney has influenced many, many people in the music biz. Here's a list of just some of those artists who have either been a fan or been influenced by the star in recent times: Nicki Minaj, Lana Del Ray, Lady Gaga, Miley Cyrus, Katy Perry, Meghan Trainor, Demi Lovato, Marina and the Diamonds, Tegan and Sara, Grimes, Selena Gomez, Hailee Steinfeld, Fergie, Porcelain Black and even Barry Manilow, who has cited Spears' personal breakdown as the inspiration for his album *15 Minutes*.

What is the Britney Army?

After bursting onto the scene in 1999 with her debut album ...*Baby One More Time*, former Mouseketeer Britney Spears, would go on to become an international pop-culture icon and, according to *Rolling Stone*, 'one of the most controversial and successful female vocalists of the twenty-first century'. With her combination of innocence and sexuality, Spears would become one of the best-selling teenage artists of all time, with her debut album selling more than 13 million copies in the United States alone. Before she had even turned twenty, she had sold more than 37 million albums, gaining a loyal following in the process.

With enduring, undeniable hits like '...Baby One More Time', 'Toxic', 'Oops! ...I Did it Again', 'Crossroads', 'Gimme More', 'Womanizer' and 'Till the World Ends', Britney obsessives have transitioned from mere fans into the more formidable Britney Army.

While there is little formal recognition of the term Britney Army, its presence on Facebook, fan sites and Twitter has made it a rallying moniker for passionate Britney die-hards all over the world.

There are few superfans more passionate than members of the Britney Army. Among their legion they count the likes of Chris Crocker, made famous by his 2007 YouTube video *Leave Britney Alone!*, in which he pleaded with Britney detractors to give the pop star personal space while she was going through her much-publicised breakdown; 'The Dollhouse Dude', who supported Britney by standing watch outside a courthouse during Britney's much-publicised custody hearing; and Bryan Ray, who has spent an estimated US$80,000 on more than 90 cosmetic procedures in order to look just like the pop princess.

So, how can you tell if you're a member of the Britney Army? Simple. You've purchased all the fragrances from her perfume line; you own and even enjoy watching the 2002 movie *Crossroads*; you're a member of a fan club Facebook page; and, more than likely, you've jumped onstage during one of her live performances.

Why you should become a member of the Britney Army...

With six MTV Video Music Awards, including the Lifetime Achievement Award, ten Billboard Music Awards, a star on the Hollywood Walk of Fame, a Grammy, and more than 100 million albums and 100 million singles sold worldwide (making her one of the best-selling musicians of all time), it's safe to say there are some pretty good reasons for becoming a member of the Britney Army already.

But Britney's legacy isn't just about her music. Britney Spears personifies popular culture – heck, she *is* pop culture. She will forever be one of the faces of the 1990s and 2000s,

and be remembered as one of the great meteoric breakouts in teen idol lore. The *Guinness World Records* lists her as the most searched-for person of the noughties.

Additionally, Britney has remained committed throughout her career to combatting bullying, and has a special interest in the welfare of LGBTQ youth. She is a regular participant of Spirit Day, an annual LGBTQ awareness day, which falls on the third Thursday in October. Spears has also donated money to the music program of John Philip Sousa Middle School, whose music studio is named in her honour.

Bruce Tramps

Bruce Springsteen

Demo

No-nonsense adults willing to drop an impractical amount of money travelling to as many concerts as humanly possible.

Signature

Being divided over just about everything – from favourite albums ans eras to politics – yet agreeing that ultimately Springsteen is their saviour.

Vibe

A Springsteen concert isn't anything like a music concert: it's more like a church service. Fans sing along and sway to the sermon, being revived and saved.

Motto

'I saw rock and roll future and its name is Bruce Springsteen.'

Who are the Bruce Tramps?

Born in 1949, New Jersey native Bruce Springsteen continues to enjoy the highs of an incredible music career spanning forty-plus years. Since releasing his first album in 1973, the rock star has gone on to sell more than 120 million records worldwide, receive 20 Grammy Awards, and be inducted into both the Songwriters Hall of Fame and the Rock and Roll Hall of Fame. Backed by the E Street Band, Springsteen, nicknamed 'The Boss' (an ironic nickname that was given to him a long time ago, to Springsteen's chagrin), has become an enduring symbol of all things working-class Americana.

The Bruce Springsteen superfan 'Tramp' stamp is derived from the lyrics of smash-hit 'Born to Run', 'tramps like us, baby we were born to run'. One of eight tracks from Springsteen's 1975 album of the same name, 'Born to Run' has been ranked at number 21 on *Rolling Stone* magazine's '500 Greatest Songs of All Time' and is included in the Rock and Roll Hall of Fame's '500 Songs that Shaped Rock and Roll'.

Like Phish and the Grateful Dead, Springsteen is known for changing up his live performances. And like those aforementioned bands, The Boss's concerts have cultivated a culture of repeat attendances, with fans following a live tour from place to place, city to city.

Additionally, Springsteen fosters his cult-like following through the connections he makes with his audience – it's a harmonious relationship. A typical Springsteen concert is more than three hours long, not bad for a performer in his late sixties. In fact Springsteen gave his longest concert in 2012, a four-hour-and-six-minute epic, which he played to a sold-out crowd in Helsinki (he played for 4:03 in 2016). Audiences tend to get their money's worth.

Superfans like Mark Ryder from Yorkshire, England, have followed Springsteen across the globe for decades – for Ryder, since 1985, when he first saw The Boss on his *Born in the USA* tour: 'I bought the t-shirt that night and I've worn it to every concert since.' That's more than 100 concerts. (The shirt now has a few holes.)

Why you should become a Bruce Tramp…

It's the intimate nature of Springsteen's relationship with his devotees, especially in the context of his live performances, that makes Tramp-dom so special. The Boss acknowledges his audience by playing to the crowd and by selecting songs based on the location he's playing in. On his recent Australian tour, for instance, Springsteen made a special effort to cover some bands from Down Under, singing classics from the likes of AC/DC, Midnight Oil and INXS.

The Boss knows his Tramps, which is why Mark Ryder isn't the only person to have seen his idol live in concert 100 times. In fact, there's a swathe of 100-plus Tramps. With so many regulars often in attendance, Bruce has come to recognise those who keep coming back, showing his appreciation by bringing them onstage to dance with him, repaying loyalty with a little kindness and a moment in the spotlight. Many of these great moments can be seen in countless videos online, including Bruce dancing with one of his oldest superfans, 91-year-old Jeanne Heintz. Heintz, like Ryder, is part of the 100 club, too. Legend has it that there's even a 400 club out there. Given Springsteen's longevity, this might just be plausible.

For all things Tramp, we suggest checking out Backstreets.com or the book *Tramps Like Us: Music and meaning among springsteen fans.* Oh, and then there's *Springsteen and I*, too, a 2013 documentary about the life and career of The Boss, which is made up entirely of fan-submitted videos.

Springsteen fandom seems to be a constant feedback loop of positivity. Writing for *Slate* magazine in 2005, critic Stephen Metcalf wrote: 'Springsteen is no longer a musician. He's a belief system. And, like any belief system worth its salt, he brooks no in-between. You're either in or you're out.'

Deadheads

Grateful Dead

Demo

Unwashed hippies reeking of patchouli oil and making a crust selling tie-dyed T-shirts and veggie burritos.

Killing joke

Q: 'What does a Deadhead say when the drugs wear off?
A: 'This music sucks!'

Known for

Getting stoned, enjoying jams. Getting stoned, enjoying jams. Getting stoned, enjoying jams.

VIP Deadheads

Famous fans of the Grateful Dead include Whoopi Goldberg, Al Gore, Steve Jobs, Walter Cronkite, Will Arnett, *Game of Thrones* author George R.R. Martin and former US Presidents Barack Obama and Bill Clinton.

Who are the Deadheads?

Founded in the San Francisco Bay Area amid the counterculture of the 1960s, the Grateful Dead would go on to enjoy a 30-year career in the music business before disbanding after the death of founding member Jerry Garcia in 1995.

In many ways, the Grateful Dead were the counterculture. They played as the house band during author Ken Kesey's infamous Acid Test parties, developing their psychedelic playing style in the process. Today, at the University of California, Santa Cruz, there is a Grateful Dead Archive, housing material received or collected by the band. Speaking on the importance of the archive, curator Nicholas Meriweather says: 'The Grateful Dead Archive is going to end up being a critical way for us to approach and understand the 1960s and the counterculture of that era.'

Just as the 1960s were integral to both the success and the identity of the Grateful Dead, their loyal fan base – the Deadheads – are more like a part of the band, rather than mere enthusiasts.

The term Deadhead originates from its 1971 appearance on the sleeve of the band's second live album, *Grateful Dead*, which read:

DEAD FREAKS UNITE:
Who are you? Where are you?
How are you?
Send us your name and address and we'll keep you informed.
Dead Heads, P.O. Box 1065,
San Rafael, California 94901

By the end of that year the band had received an estimated 350 letters from Deadheads across the United States. But the letters increased dramatically over the ensuing years, to a staggering 40,000 fan letters.

The formation of the Deadhead community was based partly on the nature and structure of the band's music, and especially their live performances. The Grateful Dead were famously idiosyncratic when it came to their concerts: their set lists changed from one night to the next; they would frequently play more than one set; and they included long sections of improvisational jams, known as 'space' jams. Such variation in music and performance lent itself to a cult following. Deadheads soon became obsessed with (dare we say paranoid about?) what they could miss out on from one concert to the next and so they began to follow the band, going on tour with them in large numbers and attending all consecutive live shows wherever they played.

Over the years the Deadhead community grew in numbers, and many of these fans still exist today, passionately following the various incarnations of the original band since Garcia's death. As drummer Mickey Hart once said, 'The Grateful Dead weren't in the music business, they were in the transportation business.'

Why you should become a Deadhead...

If you're not one already then there's some basic matters of etiquette that first need to be established. No true Deadhead wants to hear 'Truckin'', for example. You should want to hear the Grateful Dead play songs like 'Terrapin Station', 'Dire Wolf', 'Althea', 'Dark Star' or 'Scarlet Begonias'.

The point is, being a Deadhead is all about the music – about going as deep and as far into the music as humanly possible. And the same goes for the band, who, throughout their career, were dedicated to producing music for their fan base. One of the more distinguishing features of Deadhead culture is the recording of live performances on tape. 'Tapers' were practically encouraged by Jerry Garcia, who famously said of the practice when asked how he felt about it, 'When we are done [with the concerts], they can have it.' Cool words from a pretty cool guy.

As far back as 1971, the first Free Underground Grateful Dead Tape Exchange was set up to help preserve the heritage of the Grateful Dead's history of live performances by creating and exchanging copies of the tape recordings made by Deadheads. This tape exchange became a worldwide movement that still persists today – such is the community-minded spirit of Deadhead culture. Today, digital copies of these recordings can be found online, where they are freely exchanged between those concerned with spreading the good vibes of those many, many Grateful Dead concerts.

Directioners

One Direction

Signatures

Fits of jealousy where the romances of 1D members are concerned; insulting all other boy bands in the known universe.

Demo

Thirsty teens-turned-adults who can't accept that their teen idols are now adults.

Sample tweet

@devon_stratton: @Harry_Styles I wish you and Kendall break up. It is not fair and I hate Kendall she sucks a whole lot.

Hopes, dreams and aspirations

To see Justin Bieber join the band as a new fifth member, replacing Zayn.

Who are the Directioners?

When Niall Horan, Liam Payne, Louis Tomlinson, Zayn Malik and Harry Styles all auditioned for *The X Factor* as individuals, they didn't do very well at all.

But when controversial media personality and producer Simon Cowell had the brilliant idea of putting the five lads together, well ... heavenly delight!

With hits such as 'What Makes You Beautiful', 'Little Things' and 'Drag Me Down', and with their third album *Midnight Memories* being the number-one-selling album of 2013 worldwide, 1D have become quite the musical powerhouse in recent times. And, despite their recent split, the giant fan following they've generated in their six-year career still remains.

These passionate folk are known as the Directioners.

Like the Swifties, Directioners are a fan base who came up with their own moniker. As One Direction publicist Simon Jones puts it, 'The fans started the Directioners name early on in their career.' But it wasn't until band members cottoned on to the word and started using it themselves to refer to fans that the term really took off globally.

Like the band themselves, Directioners are something of a global sensation, too. They're always up to all kinds of nutty things, such as writing fan fiction, drawing lifelike illustrations of band members, copying Harry Styles' tattoos or simply tattooing Harry Styles' face onto their bodies. (Defending Harry's tatts, regardless of how you really feel about them, is a Directioner's job!)

And the fun doesn't stop there. Directioners have been known to threaten the murder of a pet dog for the worthy cause of a Twitter follow, and a particularly devoted fan was even caught stealing (and wearing) Liam Payne's boxer shorts.

But it's not all sunshine and boxer briefs. There remains real divisions in the Directioner community, too.

Two issues are particularly divisive: Zayn Malik's premature departure in 2015, and the band's *X Factor* origins. While for some fans Zayn's departure is a non-issue, others consider it a betrayal of epic proportions and make it their business to disparage his solo career. All we can say is that *Pillowtalk* makes for a pretty decent listen.

More complex, though, is the issue of Directioner purity. For an enclave of Directioners, having 'been there from the start' is a point of pride. Such fans were supporters of the lads during their very first auditions on *The X Factor* and, for these Directioners, this is a meaningful point of distinction. Anyone 'not there from the start'? Not a true Directioner.

Why you should become a Directioner...

While they're no longer together, One Direction leave behind an abundance of good tunes for any and all of us to enjoy. And, hey, life moves on. Maybe their split isn't such a bad thing after all. Directioners have to face the reality that the boys are now men and take solace in what really counts: the music.

Besides, the real benefit of being a Directioner will always remain: that Harry will always be around to save his most devoted fans. Just check out the many videos of him online, looking out for the safety of those nearest and dearest. Because despite the crushing mobs that follow him everywhere he goes, Harry always has time to help a fallen fan.

Elvis Nuts

Elvis

Vibe

Quiffs, Cadillacs and suspicious minds.

Demo

Blue suede shoe–wearing hound dogs.

Willing to forgive

The paunch, the prudishness, the patriotism (depending on where you stand).

Who are Elvis nuts?

Okay, so technically Elvis fans aren't actually called 'Elvis nuts', but they should be. When people get into Elvis, they *really* get into Elvis. Without even looking at the illustrations in this book, most of us can conjure up an image of an Elvis fan clad in a spangled, flared jumpsuit and sporting a quiff and mutton-chop sideburns.

And why is that? you might wonder. Because Elvis fans are *nuts!*

If you don't know already – and how could you not? – then Elvis Presley, nicknamed The King (as in, The King of Rock 'n' Roll), is regarded as the twentieth century's greatest pop culture icons. As one of the earliest adopters of the rockabilly style of rock music, which combines country music and rhythm and blues with a syncopated up-tempo beat, his high-energy songs and sexually provocative style of performance made him a sensation at the height of the American civil rights movement. It was Elvis' musical influences – which blended the musical styles of both black and white communities – that made him an incredibly controversial figure indeed.

The talent outweighed the controversy, however. From the launch of his career in 1953, to his death in 1977 and through to today, Elvis has sold more than 600 million records, albums, CDs and singles worldwide.

As well as being a musician, Elvis was an actor and a total heart-throb, and yet he was famously terrified of flying and often presented with the type of idiosyncratic behaviour normally associated with recluses and hermits. The end of his life was, honestly, pretty sad. He got divorced; he got fat scoffing peanut butter, bacon and banana sandwiches (an odd combination, we know); he was hooked on prescription pills; and, ultimately, he left the building for good, punching out on his bathroom floor in one of the more undignified ways a man could go (it was a heart attack, but the rumour mill has him dying on the toilet from a drug overdose).

The end was not befitting a King. Not at all. But it's all part of the legacy and the mythos now. And, quite frankly, Elvis's death is essential to Elvis fandom. Hope grips the community of those left wondering what could've been.

Elvis nuts continue to allege they've sighted The King, pointing to discrepancies in his death certificate. His death, they say, was a ruse and that a wax dummy was placed in his coffin the day he was buried before a crowd of 80,000 people. How else could a man that famous retire from his career in peace?

Why you should be an Elvis nut...

The sadness that permeates remembrances of Elvis's life and death (he was just 42 when he died), is equalled only by the resounding joy that Elvis aficionados derive from celebrating his music and legacy.

Since his passing, Elvis fanatics have done everything conceivable in the name of The King. In the Netherlands, one superfan has built an exact replica of Presley's former Graceland home, while in the States, superfan Paul MacLeod built a Graceland museum, which displayed to the public some of MacLeod's 35,000 Elvis records. Actor Nicolas Cage is also an Elvis nut, which is a large part of the reason he married

The King's daughter, Lisa Marie. Even more bizarrely, Elvis nuts have bought clippings of The King's hair at auctions, as well as any and all other personal items once owned by the rock icon.

And finally, there's those diamanté jumpsuit-wearing impersonators that seem to exist everywhere in the world. One of the most notable legacies Elvis left behind is a rich tradition of impersonators. But hey, who hasn't sung an Elvis song into the mirror, trying desperately to recreate that perfect, trembling Memphis mumble, at once so macho yet so fragile?

You know you have, and there's a great reason why. Elvis's voice didn't just ooze sensuality, it might just be *the* most iconic sound in music history in the past 100-plus years. If that sounds like a big call, then really think about it. Apart from the advent of the electric guitar, a hit song here and there, what stands out more than that quavering encapsulation of a person's soul? His voice and his voice alone might just be the greatest instrument ever produced by mankind.

Fanilows

Barry Manilow

Demo

Real housewives.

Barry

Known for

Fearsome singalongs.

Fanilows
you know

Your lovable auntie and
your sweet old nan.

Who are the Fanilows?

While Barry Manilow may not be a household name for the younger generation, the numbers do not lie: more than 40 years in the world of show biz, more than 70 million records sold, and only a single facelift required after decades of hard smiling. That's right, the 73-years-young lounge singer is looking pretty darn good these days. Most impressively, he's still doing what has always done – playing the piano for and crooning to music halls filled with legions of his adoring fans.

These fans call themselves Fanilows, a simple portmanteau that combines 'fan' with 'Manilow'. And of all the groups of superfans within the pages of this book, the Fanilows might just be the most fearsome. Don't let their age lead you to underestimate just how truly wild Baz obsessives can be.

While they may not be hip to social media, Barry's Fanilows aren't unaccustomed to participating in the occasional savage takedown of any of Manilow's online detractors. In fact, when UK-based journo Lorelei Reddin criticised a Manilow concert in one of her articles, she became the victim of some Fanilow cyber-bullying, receiving a torrent of nasty emails: 'A few Fanilows spent the bank holiday weekend abusing me for being appalling, disgusting and, the most original slight of all, a lazy journalist.'

Wow, truly shocking!

But despite their advancing years, Fanilows are a darn lively bunch – one might even say rabid, in fact. While celebrating his 72nd birthday, Manilow found his private party, held at the famed New York restaurant Trattoria Dell'Arte, crashed by two such rabid fans, who were eventually captured and removed by security.

Why you should become a Fanilow ...

Apart from the music, with hits like 'Copacabana', 'Weekend in New England', 'Looks Like We Made It', 'Ready to Take a Chance Again', 'Mandy' and 'Could It Be Magic', one of the best reasons for becoming a Fanilow is that it's exceptionally easy. Both Manilow and his Fanilows have made it that way, establishing dozens of Barry Manilow fan clubs worldwide. You could join your national Manilow fan club, or join the Barry Manilow International Fan Club, which hosts a range of events and parties.

These fan clubs have lots of get togethers. With Manilow spending so much time in Las Vegas, the fan-club parties are a way for Fanilows to get their fix of Barry music, have a couple of wines over nibbles and talk all things Barry. For the price of an admission ticket, of course. But the money is worth it. Rumour has it that Manilow sometimes dresses in drag and attends these fan-club parties incognito.

The Juggalos

Insane Clown Posse

Clown lingo

Dark Carnival, 'Whoop, whoop!',
The Riddle Box, The Great Milenko,
Hatchetman, Wicked Clown, Faygo
Shower, Joker's Cards.

VIP
Juggalos

Charlie Sheen,
Chuck D, Coolio and
Vanilla Ice.

Gang sign

The Wicked Clown hand sign is the gesture
of the Juggalo. It is made by crossing one's
arms and making the 'Westside' sign with the
left hand and forming a 'C' with the right.
The Wicked Clown sign, when displayed, is a
gesture of solidarity between Juggalos, and a
way of expressing one's standing as a member
of the Juggalo community.

Who are the Juggalos?

Insane Clown Posse, or ICP for short, is an American hardcore hip-hop duo from Detroit comprising band members Violent J (AKA The Duke of the Wicked) and Shaggy 2 Dope (AKA The Southwest Strangla). Together, ICP performs a subgenre of hip-hop known as horror-core, which emphasises darkly transgressive and horror-themed lyrical content and imagery.

While ICP's fan base fails to reach the dizzying numbers of, say, a Taylor Swift or Miley Cyrus, the duo boasts some of the most intense fans in the music fandom universe: the Juggalos (or Juggalettes, for women).

The term originated at a concert in 1994, when, during ICP's performance of the song 'The Juggla', Violent J addressed the audience as Juggalos. The positive crowd response resulted in the name sticking. Ever since, ICP members have used the word to refer to themselves, friends, family and fans.

Like all superfans, ICP obsessives are a tight-knit community, but that bond seems particularly strong between Juggalos. Their cult-like devotion to the band has birthed many idiosyncratic rituals, including spraying one another with Faygo (a cheap soft drink), wearing face paint, displaying the gesture of the Wicked Clown, having the Hatchetman logo displayed on personal items, and making and responding to the Juggalo cry of solidarity, 'Whoop, whoop!'

All of these behaviours are on display each year at the annual festival known as The Gathering of the Juggalos (or simply The Gathering to those in the know). This festival, famed in the Juggalo community, has seen artists including Ice Cube and MC Hammer perform during the multi-day affair. In 2010, an amazing 20,000 Juggalos showed up to be a part of the action.

With their shared values of family and solidarity, Juggalos don't just support each other; they also make an impact on other communities. Several charities and community-outreach programs have been organised by Juggalos including The Dead Stephanie Memorial Cleanup, Hatchet House and JMAD (Juggalos Making A Difference), a charity organisation based in Denver, Colorado.

Unfortunately, in recent years, some criminal street gangs have adopted the Juggalo name as well as associated Juggalo imagery. But, as real Juggalos know, ICP fandom has nothing to do with criminal behaviour – it's about family!

Why you should become a Juggalo ...

There's no time like the present, they say. This is especially so for ICP fans, whose loyalty to their favourite group continues to be rewarded year in and year out.

It was back in 2002, on the album *The Wraith: Shangri-La*, that ICP firstrevealed for the first time the meaning of the group's Dark Carnival mythology. 'That's when we said that the Dark Carnival was God and all that,' said Violent J of the song 'Thy Unveiling' in one interview. This same album explained that the hidden message of the band's music was to always follow God in an attempt to ascend to Heaven.

The Dark Carnival is a similar concept to the ideas of Heaven and Hell, and is detailed throughout the ICP's extensive discography from 1989 to the present. The Dark Carnival was inspired by a dream Violent J had, in which he envisioned spirits in a travelling carnival. In the ICP universe, this Dark Carnival is where human souls face judgement for their sins before being sent to Hell.

More recently, Violent J had this to say about his hopes for the future of ICP and Juggalos everywhere: 'Even though things are crazy in the world with the president, the re-emergence of racism and insanity, that's just the devil trying to rain on our parade. Let's shine. Let's beam positivity and karma and don't let hate distract you.'

To that we say a resounding *Whoop, whoop!*

KatyCats

Katy Perry

Demo

Dreamers, radio-listeners, cute-funny girls.

Known for

A deep love of cats, cat puns and all other cat-related material.

KatyCats

Savage scratchings

After NFL team the Cincinnati Bengals, announced they were no longer using KP's song 'Roar' during home games, KatyCats everywhere drew their claws and fangs, attacking the team on social media and wishing them ill for the season ahead.

Who are the KatyCats?

She was Smurfette in the 2011 film *The Smurfs* and in the 2013 sequel *The Smurfs 2*, and she was married to British comedy legend Russell Brand from 2010 to 2012. But who is *she*? The cat's mother, as our grannies used to say? Well, almost. We're talking, of course, about Katy Perry, the subject of 2012's autobiographical documentary *Katy Perry: Part of Me*, which details the trajectory of Perry's life, splicing footage from her childhood and teenage years with her performances across the globe and interviews with the megastar, as well as cameos from fellow contemporary divas such as Lady Gaga, Adele and Rihanna.

The singer of hits 'I Kissed a Girl', 'Hot n Cold', 'California Gurls', 'Firework', 'Last Friday Night (T.G.I.F.)' and 'Dark Horse' – a collection of songs that cover a broad spectrum of pop music – has lived something of a charmed life ever since her second album, *One of the Boys*, became a commercial success in 2008. Since then, Perry has accumulated a loyal following of adoring fans: the KatyCats.

Charmed by Perry's natural, bubbly personality (the funny, cute-girl persona is *not* an act, they will remind you), the KatyCats are immersed in every aspect of the singer's day-to-day life, which is how they came up with their name. The story goes that fans on a prominent Katy Perry message board were the first to coin the name, basing it on Perry's own love of cats. Not long after, Perry gave the name her seal of approval, running with it on her Twitter feed. But the most important individual to give the name a blessing was Perry's feline bestie, Kitty Purry, who gave it a solid two paws up.

Why you should become a KatyCat...

Katy Perry loves her fans. She even takes selfies with them. As in, she takes selfies with her fans, like, in the way her fans want to take selfies *with her*. That's some serious fan love, right there.

But don't just take it from us; here's one fan's thoughts on what being a KatyCat can do for you: 'This world can be harsh and cruel at times. Sometimes people feel alone, unloved or unwanted. But being a KatyCat, you feel you belong. We are a family; a big, loving, crazy, amazing family!'

And as such a family, Perry takes it upon herself to be that 'cats' mother'. Going out of her way to make her fans happy, KP proudly refers to herself as 'mom' – regardless of her KatyCats' age!

On the pop singer's leadership of the KatyCats, one fan states: 'She gives us confidence. She empowers us and encourages us to always try our best. She shows us that although life is not always perfect, and sometimes it can be very difficult, we can get through and overcome anything.'

KISS
Army

#ISS

Demo

Tongue-wagging ghouls. Catmen. Those from outer space. And all the women in the world.

How to

Easy. Rock and roll all nite (and party every day).

Signatures

Owning and collecting all available merchandise, including pinball machines, action figures, comic books and the KISS Visa credit card, which comes with customised options displaying either the entire band or your favourite member (yes, this is a real thing).

What is the KISS Army?

What do a Demon, a Starchild, a Catman and a Space Ace have in common?

Nothing, you say? Well yeah, pretty much.

There wasn't a whole lot of logic in the decision KISS members made back in 1973, when they first got together, to dress themselves in black-and-white make-up and elaborate costumes, and take on the personas of comic book–like characters. It was just that it was the seventies, man, and it was simply the done thing in a time when glitter and glam reigned supreme in the rock world.

And as one of the biggest-selling acts of the 1970s, thanks to their spectacular onstage theatrics – including Gene Simmons's iconic bass-playing, fire-breathing, tongue-wagging ghoul – it was only natural that KISS would develop a loyal following of fans.

Their fans, today, are known as the KISS Army.

But before the KISS Army became the unofficial term for KISS fanatics the world over, it was the official name for the KISS fan club.

In 1975, Bill Starkey and Jerry Evans, two teenage fans from Indiana, started contacting local radio stations in order to have KISS songs played. They would even write letters to the radio stations, signing them as 'President of the KISS Army'. Soon after, the music began to be played and radio hosts would make reference to the 'KISS Army' who had requested the songs. Before long, radio listeners were calling in, asking where they could enlist.

When KISS finally made it to Indiana for a concert, their publicist recruited Starkey and Evans to help promote the event. During the sold-outshow, KISS presented Starkey with a plaque for his efforts in helping drum up interest in the concert. And then, in 1976, a year after those first attempts to contact a local radio station, the KISS Army was made the official fan club of the band, with KISS's manager even commissioning designers to create an official logo.

To this day, the official fan group still exists, but the term has been broadened to include all KISS fans.

Why you should become a member of the KISS Army ...

Becoming a member of the KISS Army provides you with a wealth of memories to explore. Sure, there's the music, with multiple Platinum and Gold albums, and hit singles such as 'Rock and Roll All Nite', 'Shout It Out Loud', 'Beth' and 'I Was Made For Lovin' You', but the music almost pales in comparison to the real reason KISS is so well and fondly remembered: the merchandise.

KISS isn't just a band: they're a brand and an idea and a cartoon fantasy. It's what makes them so compelling. KISS fans can follow the band far outside the world of music and into an epic dream realm, with a plethora of comic books and movies to explore. In 1977, Marvel published the first KISS comic book, which sold in excess of 400,000 copies. Legend has it that the red ink used in the printing of these comics contained small amounts of blood drawn from the band members themselves. Since that time, Marvel has continued to run the series on and off. Additionally, KISS have appeared in animated movies such as *KISS Meets the Phantom of the Park*, and let's not forget Gene Simmons's hit show *Gene Simmons Family Jewels*, which ran from 2006 to 2012.

So much KISS, so little time ...

Lisztomania

Franz Liszt

Demo

Impressionable young women, particularly those who made up part of the nineteenth-century European aristocracy.

Signatures

Madness and irrepressible lust.

VIP fans

All modern concert pianists, including the world-renowned Lang Lang, who was first exposed to Liszt's music as a child while watching an episode of *Tom and Jerry*.

What was Lisztomania?

If we're talking about superfans, no discussion is complete without talking about Franz Liszt, arguably planet Earth's first rock star.

Franz Liszt was born more than 200 years ago, in 1811, in Hungary. Liszt was a pianist and, later, a composer. At the age of just nine, he gave his first concert performance and, soon after, began touring as a solo pianist. According to Lizst's contemporary and fellow concert pianist (and Lisztomaniac) Robert Taub, Liszt was a pioneer of the piano recital, helping shape it from a rather mundane affair – which it had become in the nineteenth century – to a 'high-wire event' of 'high drama'.

In the early 1800s, the polite salons of Europe were unaccustomed to Liszt's flamboyant playing style, and his audiences were unaccustomed to watching a performer play without sheet music. Today, musicians who play by memory are praised for such virtuosity, but in Liszt's era this was considered bad taste – arrogant, in fact. But Liszt didn't care. He believed that a performance needed not only music but also physical spectacle, which he achieved by placing his piano side-on to his audience so that they could watch his face as he whipped his head back and forth, sending his hair flying and shooting beads of sweat into the crowd.

As it turned out, his audiences didn't seem to mind this new playing style at all. In fact, Franz Liszt became something of a musical god. Where it had previously been considered that a solo piano performance couldn't hold the attention of an audience, Liszt's performances were so captivating that audience members – mostly women, it should be noted, for he was an extremely handsome fellow – would literally fight one another in a bid to claim a single lock of his shoulder-length hair.

The frenzy and rabid devotion that Liszt inspired in his audience was termed 'Lisztomania' by German writer Heinrich Heine. Heine had witnessed first-hand some of the Liszt devotees' impulses: behaviour that included women throwing their clothes onto the stage during his performances, as well as taking his masticated cigar butts and placing them in their cleavages.

Despite such fame and notoriety, Liszt walked away from the rock-star life, stopping touring at the age of 26 following the death of his father. He would go on to become a teacher, a composer and a conductor, and he would help shape and redefine many of these rolls too. As a teacher, he introduced the idea of the masterclass, bringing students together to learn piano and, as a conductor, he transformed the position from one that simply facilitated the performance of an orchestra into a role where, according to concert pianist Stephen Hough, 'played the orchestra as an instrument'.

Why you should become a Lisztomaniac ...

While we can no longer attack Liszt during one of his recitals like his fans did during the 1800s, we remain Lisztomniacs, all of us, nonetheless. And this is because Franz Liszt revolutionised the modern performance. If you've ever watched Liberace, Elton John or even Lady Gaga, then you've consumed a little piece of Franz Liszt and, chances are, you're a big fan. He was the first performer to stride out from the wings of a concert hall before taking his seat on stage, and the essence of Lisztomania is distilled in the way most contemporary musicians perform on stage today: seductive, captivating and dramatic. That's Liszt in a nutshell.

LISZTO♪ANIAC

Little Monsters

Lady Gaga

Handsign

The monster claw is the gesture of Little Monsters everywhere. It is achieved by splaying the fingers of one's hand apart before contorting them in an imitation of a bear's claw and making a slight slashing motion. The monster claw was demonstrated in the music video for 'Bad Romance'.

MOTHER MONSTER

Demo

All those
born this way …

Who are the Little Monsters?

What to say about an artist who once wore a dress made of raw beef? That's right, in 2010, Lady Gaga wore her now-infamous 'meat dress' to the MTV Video Music Awards as an apparent statement regarding both her distaste for the U.S. Armed Forces' policies and her beliefin one's need to always stand up and fight for what they believe in. It made such a big impression that the dress is currently preserved in the Rock and Roll Hall of Fame and has its own Wikipedia entry. Her Kermit the Frog dress probably deserves a Wikipedia page, too. In fact, so many of her outfits do.

Since her 2008 debut album, *The Fame*, Lady Gaga has produced a succession of hits, from songs like 'Just Dance' and 'Poker Face', to 'Telephone' and 'Born This Way'. Between her outrageous fashion sense and hit pop singles, it's little surprise that she has built quite the fan following over the last nine years. And, in true idiosyncratic fashion, this dazzling diva bestowed a rather unusual title upon her loyal followers: Little Monsters. As the story goes, Lady G came up with the title in the summer of 2009, while working on her album *The Fame Monster*.

There's much to learn about the world of Gaga fandom, but thanks to Gagapedia, one is able to accustom oneself to Monsterdom. There's a lot to know, but most essential of all is this: as the creator of Little Monsters everywhere, Gaga herself, holds the title of Mother Monster. A word of warning: don't get this wrong around Gaga obsessives.

Among the legion of Little Monsters, some stand out above the rest:

1) Professor Mathieu Deflam, who runs a course called Lady Gaga and The Sociology of Fame at the University of South Carolina;

2) Emma, a Gaga fan who was invited to meet Mother Monster backstage during the Born This Way Ball. Emma, who lives with scoliosis and hip dysplasia, and who bonded with Gaga during Lady G's hip surgery, has in recent times been the recipient of Mother Monster's adoration – with the star paying for her loyal fan's surgery.

3) Inez Whitfield, AKA Grandma Gaga, an 86-year-old fan who has met Mother Monster and who claims Gaga's music speaks to her in the same way The Beatles' music did decades ago.

Why you should become a Little Monster...

Lady Gaga loves her fans every bit as much as they love her. During performances, she will often stop to read letters thrown onto the stage from the crowd. She is an active mental-health campaigner, too, establishing the Born This Way Foundation, through which she encourages her Little Monsters to love themselves just the way they are in an effort to fight bullying.

The Little Monsters showed their appreciation recently, too, following criticism Gaga faced after her 2017 Super Bowl Performance. Gaga had dedicated the performance to her Little Monsters but, following the show, haters came out to bring negative attention to her body.

Not to worry, though. As it turns out, her Little Monsters are some of the most literate and grammatically correct Twitter users on the planet, and they responded to the negativity in droves:

@LMonsterReacts: Lady Gaga jumped from a stadium roof, nailed acrobatics, sang live while dancing for 13 mins, spreaded kindness, but no. BODY FUCKING SHAME!

@Chelsea_Briggs: I'm annoyed & disgusted that people would comment negatively about @ladygaga's body after her Super Bowl performance. Her bod is rockin.

@morganmahanke: If people actually think Lady Gaga was "fat" at the Super Bowl, I want to be fat. This is one community worth being part of!

Maggots
Slipknot

Known for

Moshing, stomping, rioting, losing their minds to the music.

Demo

Regardless of race, gender, class, creed, sex, shape or size, all are welcome at the altar of Slipknot worship.

Who are the Maggots?

Founded in 1995, Slipknot is a nine-piece heavy-metal band hailing from Des Moines, Iowa. With so many members, the band is able to include multiple percussionists, giving their brand of heavy metal an even more powerful and tribal sound. Slipknot are best known for their elaborate costumes, which include boiler suits and ghoulish masks, and the theatrical manner in which the band presents itself to the public. On their image, lead singer Corey Taylor said: 'It's a way of becoming more intimate with the music. It's a way for us to become unconscious of who we are and what we do outside of music. It's a way for us to kind of crawl inside it and be able to use it.'

And, speaking of unconsciousness, Slipknot have employed some pretty knock-out, bracingly bizarre methods of 'crawling inside' their music over the years. In the early days, in order to get into the right mindset before a live show, each member would sniff from a jar containing a dead bird, causing them to throw up inside their masks. Fortunately, the bird is no longer with them and the ritual has been stopped. Why, you ask? What happened to said bird? Well, according to legend, some (literally) insane fans ate the dead bird during one of Slipknot's earliest performances.

Such crazy fans deserve an equally shocking name, and in the world of Slipknot, their metal-obsessives call themselves Maggots.

Founding member Shawn 'Clown' Crahan says that Slipknot is more than a band: 'We're a culture and everybody knows it.' With Slipknot and their fans, the barrier between creator and consumer is eroded, and each party feeds off the other: 'We're one and the same, we are equal, we are together forever.' In this way, the term 'Maggot' is born from the idea that the band shares in a symbiotic relationship with its fans, feeding off them as equally as the Maggots feed off the existence of Slipknot's music.

Consequently, Slipknot have done everything possible to include the fans in their output. Notable examples include the release of an app for iOS and Android called 'Slipknot: Wear the Mask', which invited Maggots to construct their own masks that would define the type of Slipknot fans they were, and Slipknot's August 2015 show at Red Rocks, in which they encouraged fans to film their performance of 'Before I Forget'. The resultant video, cut together, can be viewed on YouTube and depicts an impressive testament to the connection between Slipknot and their Maggots, celebrating the bond the music forms between them.

But, arguably, the clearest example of the Slipknot–Maggot bond is the song 'Pulse of the Maggots', a rallying cry for the fans and ode to the highest esteem in which the band holds them.

Why you should become a Maggot...

True Maggots know they aren't just followers of a band, but are instead an essential cog in Slipknot's existence.

When shooting the video for 'Duality', Slipknot put out an open call to Maggots everywhere. Not long after, 350 fans showed up ready and willing to help the band demolish a house in Des Moines, all of which can be seen in the video today, which shows the passion and frenzy the 'Knot inspires in its devotees.

But most impressive of all was the story of a teenage lad from England who flew across the globe for the shoot with money he'd borrowed from his grandmother. After being barred from staying in a local hotel (because he was a minor), the boy was found by Corey Taylor who happened to be cruising around a local mall. The result: Taylor put the teen up in his home for the duration of the weekend.

Even if you do have to put up with the odd idiot claiming Slipknot's music is 'fake metal', it's a small price to pay for admission into one of the most welcoming fan group families in the biz. R.I.P Paul Gray.

Parrotheads

Jimmy Buffett

Demo

Lei-wearing
margarita-lovers.

Vibe

Hey, it's five o'clock
somewhere …

Price of admission

Your dignity.

Signature

Searching desperately for
a lost shaker of salt.

PARROT
IN
Paradise
HEADS

Who are the Parrotheads?

Jimmy Buffett's music, which he plays accompanied by backup group the Coral Reefer Band, has been variously referred to as 'island escapism', 'drunken Caribbean rock 'n' roll', 'gulf and western', and as a combination of 'tropical languor with country funkiness'. Whatever you want to call it, Jimmy Buffett has created one hell of an iconic sound over the years, combining folk music with country and western, and blending it all together with a cruisy, hippie/stoner (with a Caribbean twist) vibe that, while perhaps a niche, has hit it off big with flip-flop- and Hawaiian shirt-clad Baby Boomers looking to express their love of happy hours, cheeseburgers and good times.

These fans call themselves Parrotheads. (Oh, and the children of Parrotheads are called 'Parakeets', or simply 'Keets' for short. FYI.)

The term was coined in 1985 by Coral Reefer Band member Timothy B. Schmidt, after Buffett himself observed audience members wearing colourful shirts and parrot hats.

These same audience members had continuously shown up to Buffett's consecutive concerts in Cincinnati, Ohio, and were akin to Phishheads or Deadheads in their dogged determination to follow the live performances each night.

The culture of Parrotheads is steeped in a tradition of attending Buffett's live performances, before which, in parking lots outside the various venues, Buffett buffs engage in an elaborate tailgating routine. Hours before a concert, Parrotheads will fill up the car park, setting up tiki bars, inflatable pools and even pouring sand onto the asphalt before hanging out with a Landshark beer (an official Buffett-owned brand) while dressed variously in grass skirts, Hawaiian shirts and leis, or as sharks, pirates and beach bums, as well as hula girls and, yes, even a volcano. As writer Sarah Baird observed in her article about Buffett obsessives: 'Parrothead culture is cosplay that hasn't quite figured out that it's cosplay.'

Buffett's most *super* of superfans, known to the world as 'The Numbers People' (a nickname bestowed upon them by JB himself), attend these tailgate parties before concerts like every other Parrothead, but they distinguish themselves by also wearing a number, stencilled on themselves with temporary ink, to display the number of times they have seen Buffett live. The top dog of these fans is a man named Mike 'Hollywood' Holly, who has been to more than 160 Buffett shows.

Why you should become a Parrothead ...

In 2016, Jimmy Buffett made a cameo appearance in the film *Jurassic World*. There's your reason, right there. He can be seen holding two margaritas as the dinosaurs are let loose.

If that's not enough of a testament to his global popularity and recognition, Jimmy also happens to own a restaurant chain called Margaritaville, named after his hit song 'Margaritaville'. At Margaritaville an average Parrothead can enjoy a number of Buffett-themed cocktails, from a Surfing in a Hurricane to a Fins 2 The Left. Or, hungry Parrotheads might help

themselves to a bowl of Jimmy's Jammin' Jambalaya. The restaurant boasts store locations worldwide.

But if you're not a movie buff(ett), or you're unsure about consuming a cheeseburger in paradise and still need a good reason to become a Parrothead, then how about simply because they're a charitable bunch. Every year, up to 3500 Parrotheads meet at an event in Key West, Florida, called the Meeting of the Minds. The event includes live music, a toy and blood drive, a walk for breast cancer and a whole host of other events aimed at raising money for charities.

And with more than 240 Parrothead Club chapters across the globe – boasting an impressive number of members (at least 28,000, we're told) – you can become one of the many Parrotheads that have helped raise a collective US$25 million for environmental causes, Alzheimer's and cancer research, and other charitable organisations.

Phishheads

Phish

Demo

Hemp-wearing,
hacky-sack stoners
turned corporate
sell-outs.

Known for

Organisational skills where
concert attendance and
debriefs are concerned.
Obsessing over setlists.

Killing joke

Q: What's another name for Phish?
A: The Grateful Dead, but worse!

Who are the Phishheads?

Since forming in 1983, Phish have been known for their musical improvisation, extended jams and their blend of genres including funk, progressive rock, psych rock, folk, country, jazz, blues, bluegrass and pop.

And, of course, for their army of dedicated fans, known to the world as Phishheads.

The origin of the term Phishhead, much like Deadhead (pages 36–39) is simple: the band's name, plus the suffix 'head', which in this context means 'enthusiast'. In fact, both the Grateful Dead and Phish, and their fans, have a number of things in common, most notably the bands' flexible routines during live performances, their propensity for long improvisational moments, and the obsessiveness of their fans, which such a playing style seems to encourage. It's little wonder then that Trey Anastasio, Phish's scruffy frontman, joined the Grateful Dead during their reunion shows in recent years, taking Jerry Garcia's former position in the line-up.

But let's cut right to the key indicator of a Phishhead: madness!

Phish obsessives take their obsessiveness to extreme levels, spending their salaries on a year-long schedule of flights, hotels, tickets and signed concert posters as they follow the group from live performance to live performance.

In the words of comedians Key and Peele, 'When dudes get into Phish, they don't come back.' The average Phishhead doesn't just attend one concert when the troupe comes to town, no; like Deadheads, he (or she – but generally *he*) will attend all the concerts, because each set is different' each set is a perfectly crafted work of art in and of itself. And when a Phishhead isn't travelling to be at a concert in person, he's live-streaming that concert at home and raising a beer from the comfort of his sofa to Trey's profound words – words like 'wombat' and 'Wil-son' and 'Whatever you do, take care of your shoes.' Yeah, that's right, *madness.*

Additionally, a Phish concert isn't over when the noodling ends. No, no, no. For the average Phishhead, the end of a concert marks only the beginning of the next great part: meticulously going over the setlist the following morning with other Phishheads online, which, of course, requires the involvement of Mr Miner, a preeminent setlist analyst and blogger of all things Phish. No concert is complete without this ritual of morning-after reflection and analysis.

Madness …

Why you should become a Phishhead…

Like the Grateful Dead, Phish's cultural impact is immeasurable.

Each year they host their annual New Year's Eve Concert, usually performed in Madison Square Garden, to which Phishheads flock in droves, perhaps hoping to share a New Year's kiss with … Trey? The concert has the propensity to get a little rowdy. In 2014, 200 people were arrested over the four-night run at MSG, mostly for possession or sale of drugs. So, for anyone who loves drugs, poor hygiene and hours of meandering, aimless jamming – oh, and lots and lots of terrible dancing – this is the place to be.

But for those who prefer to spend their New Year's parties with non-Phish fanatics, there's always ice cream. Ben and Jerry's ice-cream flavour Phish Food is named in honour of the band, recognising the ice-cream company's and the band members' shared Vermont heritage. All of Phish's share of the proceeds from this flavour are donated towards environmental work to restore Lake Champion, a natural freshwater lake in North America. The flavour is made up of chocolate ice cream with marshmallows, caramel and fish-shaped chocolate chips.

So much goodness …

Punkers?
Robots?
Dafties?

Daft Punk

Demo

Robots. Helmet
enthusiasts. Ravers.

Signatures

Making their own helmets to
look like the band. Posting
videos detailing the process of
robot helmet making.

The price of admission

Putting up with the fact
their beloved music duo
rarely tour anymore.

Who are these robot-lovers?

Okay, okay, so first things first. Daft Punk fans don't really have a collective name, but they should. 'Daft Punkers', 'Punkers', 'Robots' and the fabulous 'Humans After All', which references the title of the duo's 2005 studio album, have all been suggested as potential monikers in online forums and message boards. Humans After All might just be the best here, as it uses the music that the fans love to influence what they call themselves, just like Eminem's 'Stans'. Such a hat-tip, we think, is most certainly moniker worthy.

Formed in 1993, Daft Punk (the name comes from a review of the song 'Cindy, So Loud', which referred to it as 'daft punky thrash'), first found success as part of the French house movement of the late 1990s. Comprised of Guy-Manuel de Homem-Christo and Thomas Bangalter, the pair are known for their visual stylisation and their disguises. Famously reclusive and interview-shy – they rarely grant them, and don't make a habit of being shown on TV – neither have been seen unmasked since 1996, instead making public appearances obscured by ornate helmets and gloves, assuming the robot personas that define Daft Punk's aesthetic. And, with 2001's smash-hit album *Discovery*, the techno duo burst onto the world stage, amassing a loyal legion of enthusiasts.

The culture of Daft Punk fandom is not nearly as bizarre as the band itself, however. For the most part, Punkers are just people that enjoy a good house track.

But that isn't to say there aren't some obsessives that stand head-and-shoulders above the rest. Take the Parisian Djamel, for instance, better known in the world of music superfandom as Daftworld. Daftworld, an avid blogger on all things Daft Punk–related, is one of the most informed sources when it comes to news and information relating to the band. Apart from his massive Facebook following, most of them Punkers looking for band-related updates, Daftworld boasts an impressive collection Daft Punk paraphernalia, including a variety of merchandise such as posters, wallets, T-shirts, art and games, as well as an extensive CD and record collection estimated to be worth more than €10,000. Naturally, he sports a few Daft Punk tattoos as well; he says he plans to get a new one at least every five years.

Why you should become a Daftie...

With Daft Punk's recent lack of tours, being a Daftie hasn't been much of a party. But fans of the robot duo have found some solace in one another and the spirit of the music.

For Punkers Eugene and James, the current touring schedule is of little consequence, preferring instead to be inspired by the essence of Daft Punk's music. The Irish lads formed a tribute band called Daft As Punk, creating an accessible Daft Punk substitute for fans to find and enjoy for only €10.

Otherwise, you can simply watch *Interstella 5555: The 5tory of the 5ecret 5tar 5ystem* a whole bunch of times on repeat. It's just your average watch, really, a Japanese-French animated-adventure-fantasy-sci-fi-musical about the abduction and rescue of an interstellar pop band that acts as a visual realisation of Daft Punk's *Discovery* album. You know, that kind of movie …

Rihanna Navy

Rihanna

Navy
no-no

Listening to
Chris Brown.

Signatures

Vicious online assaults;
loving terrible Hasbro-
inspired blockbusters.

Scripture

@rihanna: We're an Army,
better yet a Navy,
better yet CRAZY!!!

What is the Rihanna Navy?

Born in Barbados in 1988, Robyn Rihanna Fenty, or simply Rihanna as she is known today, has spent only a little over a decade making records – and yet her history of chart-topping hits such as 'SOS', 'Umbrella', 'Don't Stop the Music', 'Only Girl (In the World)', 'We Found Love', 'FourFiveSeconds' and 'Work' has already created a legacy to rival the legacies of music greats who have been going at it twice as long.

Rihanna first began referring to her fan base as her Navy after starring in the critically panned military sci-fi action flick *Battleship*. The 2012 film was actually based on the board game that shares its name; in it, Rihanna plays a Naval officer. But while *Battleship* may have sunk without a trace, Rihanna's fans salvaged their new name from the wreckage, giving life to their new moniker via their countless fan sites, Twitter accounts and Tumblr pages.

And RiRi is more than grateful for the support they've shown, too. Before the launch of her album *Unapologetic,* she penned her Navy a heartfelt handwritten letter, which was, um, totally not a marketing gimmick engineered to boost the sales of an album initially deemed to be underperforming by the music studio. No, that would be way too cynical.

We, like everyone out there, ought to watch what we say about the pop diva. After all, the Navy has some serious firepower. When they're all on board for a unified cause, it's impressive what they can achieve – we're talking crashing sites speaking ill of Rihanna, getting songs to #1 on iTunes, and the death threats Chris Brown's new girlfriends keep receiving, too … *Yikes!*

But the craziness doesn't stop there. Rather, it starts and ends with superfan Sarah Ridge from Wiltshire, England, who has spent more than £1,000 on RiRi-related tattoos, including seven tattoos of the singer's face. Ms Ridge's back is covered in a collage of tattooed images of her idol (this piece alone accounts for five of the seven Rihanna faces).

Ms Ridge also sports several replicas of Rihanna's own tattoos, including the winged Egyptian goddess Isis across her lower ribcage (okay, underboob), which Ri-Ri had done in honour of her grandmother.

Oh, and there was also a fan who broke into Rihanna's house and slept in her bed one time, but the less said about that the better.

Why you should join the Rihanna Navy...

It's not all about the craziness. It's about the love and honesty that Rihanna's music provokes, too. With such inspiring lyrics as 'pour it up, pour it up, that's how we ball out' and 'na na na, come on, na na na, come on', it only makes sense that RiRi obsessives should want to, say, create an unauthorised stage play about the singer's life that tells her story through a mix of her songs and interview quotes.

This quasi-musical *thing*, described as a 'concert with dialogue' and entitled *Good Girl Gone Bad*, is a legitimate superfan generated ode to the singer's life. And, in putting together the production, those Navy members involved might just have invented a brand new subcategory of entertainment: the 'bioconcert'. Look it up, it's going to be a thing now … we're pretty sure.

But, if you're interested in a more pure and unadulterated insight into serious Rihanna fandom, then look no further than the recently released 'Goodnight Gotham' video, in which Rihanna shows up in Paris to embrace a horde of adoring Navy members, who swarm her with cuddles before lifting her onto their shoulders in Trocadero Square. Only a diamond this bright could take some of the shine away from the City of Lights.

When asked what it was Rihanna and her music meant to the Navy, one superfan responded: 'She knows how to remain simple while being a Queen and that's why we love her. Since 2005, Rihanna taught us not to worry about what others think and it's probably what makes the strength of the Navy.'

Smilers

Miley Cyrus

Vibe

Tweenage
angst.

Demo

Hannah Montana
wrecking balls that just
can't stop.

Ideology

Smiling.

VIP Smiler

Kanye West.

Who are the Smilers?

When Destiny Hope Cyrus was born, the child was such a happy baby that her parents found themselves calling her Smiley. Not long after that, Smiley became Miley, and the rest, as they say, is history. Fans of the one-time Disney wunderkind Hannah Montana (turned Queen of Twerk) have named themselves for that happy baby, calling themselves the Smilers.

So, who are the Smilers, you ask? Well, they are at least some of the huge following Miley boasts on Twitter, and their idol loves them every bit as much as they love her. In 2015, Miley released her fifth studio album, titled *Miley Cyrus & Her Dead Petz*, for free online, which for a Smiler was cause for celebration – a cause for a Party in the USA, dare we say?

At their core, though, the Smilers are a loving group, always ready to embrace change and difference. As one Smiler put it: 'One word could describe us very well: transition.' Since jumping on the Cyrus bandwagon in 2006, Smilers have had to transition with their idol, who has gone from the sweet Hannah Montana persona to the more outrageous, explosive and sexually-charged Miley of today. But these transitions, says this same Smiler, have all been positive, as Miley's diverse career has 'taught us that we shouldn't be afraid to show who we really are, to be true to ourselves.' And this is exactly why Smilers love Miley. It isn't simply that she can rock any kind of music, whether it be pop, country, hip-hop or even dubstep; it's because she isn't fake and she isn't afraid of being different. 'This is a movement, so we are going to keep this evolution going and will support Miley 'til the end.'

This is not to say, however, that Miley's changes in career direction these past ten years have been embraced by all. The ebb and flow of the pop princess's career has been divisive to say the least. For some Smilers, 'old Miley' versus 'new Miley' is a point of contention and frustration – even resentment.

Take 42-year-old Carl McCoid, for instance. Carl, who runs an ironing business from his home in Bridlington, a small town in Yorkshire, England, found himself at something of a crossroads back in 2009 while going through a painful divorce. The Smiler and father of three daughters (one named Miley) found something like salvation during this time in what can only be described as a macabre form of therapy. Carl began spending his pocket change on tattoos, each one dedicated to showing the young singer 'how special she actually was as a person and as an idol'. Early on, Carl's hope was to attract Miley's attention via Twitter: 'That way I could actually end up meeting her. If I did, then I would die. I would definitely die.'

From 2010 to 2016, Mr McCoid spent almost £3,000 having 29 Miley-related tattoos (including song lyrics, album titles, autographs and portraits) inked onto his body. But a combination of dissatisfaction with Miley's career direction and insults from fellow Miley enthusiasts ultimately has caused him to leave the Smiler life behind. 'She used to be the girl next door, but she's losing a lot of fans,' said Carl of Miley's 'shocking and provocative behaviour', which included her 2013 MTV Awards performance, during which she infamously twerked in front of singer Robin Thicke.

Carl is currently in the process of having his tattoos removed …

Why you should become a Smiler…

If you're anything like Miley Cyrus – genderfluid, friend of the LGBTQI community, an advocate for abolishing the traditional gender paradigm and establishing transgender and gender-expansive stories – or just happen to really like pets, then becoming a Smiler is for you.

Stans

Eminem

Legacy

Turning a legion of white Gen-Y males onto rap music.

Demo

Sweater-wearing B-boys covered in mom's spaghetti.

B-RABBIT

Signature

Vehemently denouncing the idea that any other rapper in the world might be better than, or even as good as, Eminem.

Hopes, dreams and aspirations

To be the subject of an Eminem song.

Who are the Stans?

When Missouri-born rapper Marshall Bruce Mathers III, known by the stage name Eminem, released his song Stan on December 4, 2000, he unwittingly created a new word that would come to define 'superfan' all over the world.

The four-verse song, which samples lines from Dido's hit single 'Thank You', tells the story of an obsessive Eminem fan who attempts to contact and communicate with his hip-hop idol. When, in the song, Eminem does not respond promptly to Stan's repeated requests and attempts to develop a mutual rapport, Stan commits suicide by driving his car off of a bridge and into a large body of water. In the song, not only does Stan kill himself, but he murders his pregnant girlfriend, too, who he has bound and trapped in the trunk of his car.

Despite the song's graphic content and its downbeat ending, 'Stan' was a smash hit with both critics and fans. In 2001, Eminem performed the song live at the 43rd Annual Grammy Awards ceremony, with Elton John playing piano and singing the sampled Dido lyrics. (This performance is notable for the fact that, at the time, Eminem had come up against criticism from GLAAD for his use of lyrics deemed homophobic. John made a point by sticking by the young artist concerning this issue.)

And again, despite the song's subject, Stan, which works as a portmanteau of 'stalker' and 'fan', was embraced by Eminem superfans, who welcomed an association with the name.

In many ways, of all the superfan group names, Stan is the most perfect embodiment of music fans creating an identity from the work of the artist they worship, encapsulating an idealistic harmony between creator and consumer.

However, it should be noted that because 'Stan' outlines the story of a crazed and clingy fan, the term has also been applied to anyone who fits this mould. Stan is often used to describe insane fans of athletes and other artists, actors and musicians, gaining a broader definition of 'stalker-fan' and becoming part of the lexicon within forums dedicated to discussing star worship.

Why you should become a Stan...

Given that today Stan continues to morph into a more common term for an over-obsessed fan of any description, chances are you're quite possibly a Stan of something or someone already, not necessarily Eminem. (Take note: the majority of fans in this book, for instance, *are* Stans.)

But, if you need a reason to become an Eminem Stan, then how does 'best-selling artist of the 2000s in the United States' sound?

No? Why not try: 'More than 100 million albums sold worldwide'.

There's a reason they love Marshall Mathers, you know: he's a no-nonsense, brazen rebel, and his image has been one of defiant underdog since his earliest days making music.

So, get on board already.

Swifties

Taylor Swift

Taylor Swift ✓
@taylorswift13s

Known for

Wanting nothing more than to meet Taylor Swift in person: spending every waking moment swapping pictures of Taylor Swift online or attempting to get Taylor to follow them on Twitter; drawing pictures of Taylor Swift's cats … you get the idea.

Demo

Everyone …

Who are the Swifties?

The Swifties are what Taylor Swift fans call themselves. There's no great origin story here, just that in its own brilliantly banal way, the title is a model of perfect simplicity.

There is, however, some debate surrounding the spelling of the name: whether one should employ an 'ie' (Swiftie) or a 'y' (Swifty). Additionally, this difference in spelling is thought to denote a difference in the meaning and interpretation of what type of Taylor Swift superfan you really are.

But don't take it from us. Online, among the superfans debating the minutiae of Tay's music and lifestyle, the words of one informed source rang out loudest of all. This person defined a 'Swiftie' as the following:

'(Noun.) Someone who fangirls over Taylor Swift every time they see her or hear her name. They are beautiful souls who have a big heart and always treat everyone respectfully. Referred to as 'The Swifties'. Best fan base ever!'

According to this same expert, a 'Swifty', on the other hand, was:

'A girl who is completely obsessed with country singer Taylor Swift. Usually a little bit lesbian towards her, and would give anything to meet her and be like her. Supports her 100% and loves her an unhealthy amount.'

But such gender-exclusive definitions of Swift's fan base were met with these responses by 'Swiftie' self-identifying males:

Hooker321: This is hooker AKA Robert The biggest Taylor Swift fan in Wheaton Illinois and I know every single word and breath to almost all the songs but I'm a guy all the definitions to Swifty mention girl.

Swiftie25: I'm a boy Swiftie since 2007 and damn! Proud.

Alexandergoozonghan: Assuming you don't have to be a girl to be a swifty, I'm a Swiftie and swifty, but I prefer Swiftie, it's how it's always spelt as.

Controversy reigns in this community of highly literate intellectuals, but ultimately, we must turn to Tay and her team of managers in order to help put to rest the issue of official spelling. Luckily, Taylor has become active in her own fandom and attempted to trademark both the words 'Swiftie' and 'Swifties', which says to us that 'ie' is canon.

Spelling aside, what really defines a Swiftie is the obsessive madness, indicated by the following Tweets:

@**TSwiftNeedsYou**: Do you ever get emotional bc Taylor really does exist bc same

@**watchedyouleave**: If Taylor is in LA right now I will puke because it makes me nervous like what if I randomly run into her ID DIE

@**Lyyssaaaa13**: If/When I meet Taylor can I have a camera crew there so I can play it that day at my funeral cause I'll die #ripme #tswillkillme

@**selenasbieber**: I had a dream that I DIED and that heaven was a never ending taylor swift meet and greet and HELL was an airport with NO WIFI

@**starlit_swift**: I WAS GONNA SLEEP AT A NORMAL HOUR TONIGHT THEN TAYLOR DECIDED TO KILL ME BUT ITS OKAY I LIVE FOR THE THRILL

Why you should become a Swiftie...

If you like drawing pictures of Taylor's cats and posting them online, whether to Instagram or Tumblr, then you're a Swiftie already. If you enjoy long ocean swims, you have another valid reason to love this pop star. Because, as a 22-year-old gentleman from Chicago found out, swimming to Tay's Rhode Island beach home (at two o'clock in the morning and in freezing water, no less) is a sublime way to get in shape, if not to meet the singer in person. Though he was arrested for trespassing in the end, his aquatic demonstration proves something essential about the phenomenon that is Taylor Swift – and this is that we're all Swifties deep down, right?

The Victims

The Killers

Demo

Gen Ys who chose 'Hot Fuss' over 'A Rush of Blood to the Head'.

Signature

Pilgrimages to Sam's Town.

THE KILLERS and the VICTIMS NEVADA

Price of admission

An official t-shirt.

Who are
The Victims?

The Killers' name is derived from a music video for the New Order song 'Crystal', which came out in 2001, the same year The Killers formed. In the New Order video, a fictitious band named 'The Killers' performs the song – the band's name seen seen clearly embossed on the bass drum.

But, while 'Crystal' was a hit in 2001, with 22 million records sold worldwide, The Killers have done more than enough to stand apart from an obscure reference to a New Order song. In fact, *Noisey*, Vice Media's online music magazine, christened smash-hit single 'Mr Brightside' as the Millennial 'Stairway to Heaven'. And, while his might seem a frivolous honour to some, it speaks to the band's wide-reaching popularity and the place their music holds in the hearts of many Gen Ys.

Having played live in more than 50 countries across six continents, The Killers have amassed an army of loyal devotees. These superfans call themselves The Victims, a jokey reference to the notion that they have been slayed by the music – by hits such as 'Somebody Told Me', 'When You Were Young', 'Human', 'Read My Mind' and 'Bones'. It's kind of sweet, when you think about it.

The Victims community has a strong online presence, too. Like other fan bases, they're frequent posters to and users of social media. There are even guides to be found online, walking Victims through tours of Las Vegas for those interested to learn more about the city from which their favourite band originates. In many ways, the city of Las Vegas has become a Mecca for Victims dying to spend time in the Nevada heartland, where they believe they might just catch a glimpse of what makes their idols' music oh-so special.

Pilgrimage destinations include: The Hard Rock Hotel, where the skeletons from the 'Bones' music video are on display; the Aladdin Hotel, where all of The Killers used to work before making it big in the music biz; and, of course, a couple of frontman Brandon Flowers' favourite eateries, Luv-It Frozen Custard and Sushi Rocku. #FlowersFriday everyone!

The Killers' official fan club is The Victims Club (an ominous name, when you think about it). The club gives long-standing members access to pre-sale tickets for concerts as well as a host of other benefits. You will likely find these Victims Club members at concerts, where they distinguish themselves by donning their official The Victims T-shirts.

Why you should become a Victim ...

Okay, so the above phrasing might sound a little off, but don't get triggered yet. Becoming a member of The Victims is a noble and worthy cause. Like the band itself, The Victims stand for many of the charitable causes The Killers' have supported with their music over the years. And while their name may not reflect it upon first glance, The Killers

have proven they have a heart.

Since 2006, The Killers have released annual Christmas singles in aid of Product Red, a charity that supports a global fund to combat AIDS, malaria and tuberculosis. The proceeds from these songs, largely drummed up by The Victims themselves, have helped raise more than US$1 million for Product Red.

But the causes don't stop there. The Killers have made efforts to support charities and organisations that both promote an awareness of and act to combat a multitude of global political and social issues, including sex trafficking, the climate crisis, natural disasters and famine.

The Victims are with them every step of the way.

Bossy

MOTHER MONSTER

LADY GAGA / JOANNE

THE KILLERS and the VICTIMS
NEVADA

NAVY

RIRI

Justin Bieber

NEVER SAY NEVER

BELIEBER

Katy Cats

WE ♥ THE BEATLES

I WANT TO HOLD YOUR HAND JOHN!

POLICE LINE — DO NOT CROSS

QUEEN BEY

QUEEN BEY

▶ ▶❙ 🔊 1:53 / 4:17   ⚙ ▭ ⛶

Leave Britney Alone

About
the Author

Tobias Anthony is an author and writing teacher living in Melbourne, Australia. He holds a PhD in Creative Writing, which is another way of saying he wasted his formative years in the library.

Anthony's other titles with Smith Street Books include *Hipster Baby Names* (2016), *Should I Buy This Book?: Life's hardest decisions made easy by flow chart* (2017) and *Ginger Pride* (2018).

Published in 2018 by Smith Street Books
Collingwood | Melbourne | Australia
smithstreetbooks.com

ISBN: 978-1-925418-50-7

CIP data is available from the National Library of Australia

Publisher: Paul McNally
Project manager: Hannah Koelmeyer
Editor: Andrea O'Connor
Design concept: Stephanie Spartels
Design layout: Heather Menzies, Studio31 Graphics
Illustrator: Eliza Wilson

Printed & bound in China by C&C Offset Printing Co., Ltd.

Book 61
10 9 8 7 6 5 4 3 2 1